# Pictorial Journeys

Note of Thanks
I would like to thank Carolyn and Klaus
for the help they have kindly provided.

Poetry plays with words in order to recreate the world. The common factor in poems and paintings is that they make visible what we have never seen.

Poems by Evelyn Rheydt are like pictures in which words come to life. Her words live in the images of language. But they reveal more than we already know, more than just our own emotions, more than merely familiar feelings. Between the lines, they quietly express a hesitation, an emptiness in which the flow of beautiful words threatens to die off. There is a sudden, unexpected hint of terror, of time that cannot be repeated, a farewell, a fracture.

For Evelyn Rheydt, taking leave is the beginning of words. This is how she describes what she saw before her eyes. But she can not, and does not want to, bring it back. Homesickness is foreseeable, because the question remains of where we are at home. In memories of what is lost? Or in the new world of words, in poetry?

With the quiet, careful soberness of her descriptive language, Evelyn Rheydt does not stifle the pain of loss with feelings of unity. On the contrary, she often reveals a little of the melancholy of life. That is why her poems fascinate, not just because we savour her aesthetic way with words. Evelyn Rheydt keeps her feelings in check so that we are free enough to engage with the poems instead of with feelings. This way there is scope to see the unseen, to hear the unheard above all scope to achieve a distance from oneself. The poems have their own view of things. How true is their perception?

Evelyn Rheydt's poetry gives her experiences a language we can appreciate, words that engage us. They are reflective, thoughtful, sometimes meditative, sometimes challengingly direct. The eroticism of the words attracts us. At the same time we are aware of what we are constantly losing. There is a vision here that what we have lost could hold the promise of a new life.
Homesickness foreseeable. Homesickness for the poetry of life.

Professor Dr. Dietrich Zilleßen
University of Cologne

# Pictorial Journeys

## Poems

## Evelyn Rheydt

## Foreign City

early in the morning
the shrill cries
of the swallows
echo in the streets

in the far distance
city traffic roars

never ending grey
days are stretching
in gloominess
the sky is pressing leaden
on the world

when will sunlight
float again
through the pale cold world
awakens the birds' joyful singing

the sky is black of blue
lines shimmering like diamonds
create cool shadows

warmth vibrates over the snow

## At the Window

the clear cold turquoise
of the evening sky
changes slowly
into a smooth pink grey
takes the brightness
from the snow away

regrets arise
about the time
turned already
into memory

ill looking green of the meadows
in winter-dirty March
leaden deep skies
over blue-black leafless trees

waiting for spring

## Morning in May

silence
nothing to hear
but the songs of the birds

two black points
are seen on the horizon
race nearer in a rush
rend the sky
like gigantic black missiles

after them
the silence
smashes
shatters
breaks into pieces

## On the River

fragrance of meadows
earthly redolence
the aspen whisper
brown the muddy river
shining green tree reflection
jubilant birds
a cuckoo call
dancing yellow wings
of butterflies
smoothly gliding
down the river
early morning
Sunday's silence
no longing
no wishes

## Lake Como

mountains rise
in oppressive haze
on the horizon
marking the lake
the water moves unsteadily
damp heat lies over all

wind carries delicately
sounds of an unknown melody
over the hedge
into my dreams

thoughts full of fantasy
revolve around
the new home
the foreign land

homesickness foreseeable

dirty grey waves eat into
magnificent crumbling facades
heat covers the reflection

disturbing fragrances
mixed by all possibilities

neglect and splendour
combined with uniqueness

Venice

aged depraved queen

## Vinci

spring embraces
the old house
on the slope
with gaudy red poppies
and silver shady olive trees

memory comes back
awakes the pain
of jealousy anew
which covers the walls
like mildew
since last year

## Farewell

dust interwoven with gold
lies over the valley
in the afternoon
smoothes the sharp edges
of the mountains
into bluish lines
rising from terraced formations
from far below

a sunbeam hits a window
on the slope
makes it flash in the dust
gives the impression of a village

## Witch Judges

the ceiling blackened by age
arches over panelled walls
in a restaurant in the Alps

out of their old frames on the wall
the gentlemen
look self-satisfied
upon the guests in the room
enjoying their evening

## Driving through North Germany

shiny clear springtime blue
within the clouds are sailing
glaring yellow of rape
bright green rhythm of fields
passing by
churches rise over villages

wind blades rotate
in uneven play
on slim poles

## On the Beach

full of sand
stretches endlessness
under the wind
towards the horizon
where it immerses
into a cloud-ruffled sky

I can only laugh
at the pouring rain
when the grey liquid
runs over me

I am not bothered

I am in love

## Snap Shot

veils of birch leaves
speckled with sunrays
swaying in the wind
pinkish heather
flooding over the sand

## Tourists

through narrow streets
full of history
strolls the colourful crowd
over steps
smoothed by age

searching
for the moment
of happiness

## Facing towards Gomera

black lava rocks
plunge steep into the ocean
open up an outlook

in the far distance
rises the vague
dark mountaintop
of an island
out of the haze
lies like a ship
in the white
waves of clouds
floating
promising

pictures like this
create visions
give explorer
the urge to go

## Casa Vieja

friendly lies the old house
in between the lush green garden
peacefully idle the days away

at night
the house tells its stories
in returning urgency

## Vacation

empty days
strung like pearls
on a ribbon
rampant lush green
surrounds the house

the gaze roams
from the window
to the horizon
where the ocean
promises wide open space

## Island

white waves rush
on black beaches
gardens full of splendour
blue mountains swim
in hazy light

bright swords of sun
over lava fields
massed black clouds
gather on the horizon
repulsive ugliness
of lined up bodies
on the beach

well formed
mahaghoni coloured
floats the boat
along the high reeds
onto the grey-white water
where the wind
grips the sails
forces a fast ride
on the boat
sharply tilted
approaching
the critical moment

## Back Again

driving down the road
each corner keeps a memory
old feelings start to fade
overwhelmed by new impressions

## Evening

soft orange
cloud's grey

the last light of the day
reflects metallic in the waves
which approach the shore
continually with no rest

short moment of concentration
preparing for the night

## Sweden

spring
full of apple blossoms
given as a gift
for the second time

my joy
awakes suggestions
of something long forgotten
in my companion

thoughtless words destroy
the moment's harmony

the southern night
the gleaming waves
the silver moonlight

they have no significance
for me anymore

## Beauty

beauty
which touches me deeply

beauty
which makes my heart ache

beauty
so glorious and overwhelming

I would love to fill my heart
with all that beauty

only to send it off again

## Wide Open Space

stretch
into the blue
let drop
the limitations
open yourself
to meet
the imponderability

## Heroin

last sunlight lies over the bay
stripes brightly
the chapel on the slope aglow
happy about this beauty
the man bends over the wall
sees two young men on their way
into different worlds

# Transatlantic Flight

void
between farewell
and return

## An Evening in Boston

bluish reflecting window rows
piled up into the sky
in the grey evening twilight

wrapped in the warm light of a lamp
stands small and forlorn
a young man in the entrance
and elicits from his violin
sounds of joyful ease

## James River

old trees arch
over the river
bright green bushes
reflect on the water
golden green plants
sway in the current
like mermaid's hair
blue eyed dragonflies
quiver over the surface
a fragile leaf
sails by
steadily

the river doesn't care
about the world's tragedies

## Deep South

soft warm night
huge lanterns
attract insects
with their light
slender white columns
reach two stories high
a variety of shrill voices
keeps the night alive
magnificent fragrances
rise from bushes

on the horizon
lightning pierces the sky

## Virginia

the surface of the pool
ripples in the splendid breeze
old trees stretch out green branches

the old mansion dreams
under an ivy blanket
lulled by a hazy sun

the beauty is unchanged
why am I so moody

## Waterfall

wild white water
gushes quickly
over green mossy rocks
spreads over edges
down into the valley

the water's energetic sound
echoes deep into my body

## In a Foreign Wood

the warm sunny morning
changes into a damp grey noon
drops fall on the ground
evaporate on smooth rocks
huge unknown trees
elicit incense fragrance
turn the moment
into a celebration

the street winds
small and narrow
through the forest
up and down the hills

trees are glowing
with burning red
and shiny yellow
a waving brilliant ocean
of endless colours

sadness clouds the sight
for the autumn
in its magnificent abundance

## Prince William Sound Alaska

rising and sinking of the boat
rhythmic dance with the waves
a fresh breeze on my face
northern blue sky over the coastline
mountains polished by storms
covered with moss
in the ravines remains of snow

I smell
taste
the wind
the ocean

# Mesa Verde

round dark room
full of secrets

people dance pounding
in this ceremony hall
go round in circles
when rhythm peaks
with ecstasy

shadows flicker ghostly
over blackened walls
float back and forth
with the waves of music
deep in the earth
deep in the kiva
deep in the sacred room

## Las Vegas

the city
in the afternoon
grey dull empty

its real face
shows at night
cascades of glittering light
run up and down the facades
fictitious worlds
greedy
superficial
like the players' faces

## California

contrasts break out
deep down in the sequoia woods
between high old trees
alone
shivering from cool dampness

## Mission Church

colourful
bright walls

singing of birds
in the roof timbers

don't cover
the touch
of cruelty
and ignorance

heavy raindrops
meet the sun baked street
unique fragrance
of damp dusty asphalt
fills the air this instant

## Cotton Wood Road

grey blue earth
frozen into dunes
heaps up
to white rocks
the cracks filled
with deep red sand
the black green
of the pines
completes the colour harmony
a dream world
created to confirm
fantasies

## Slotcanyon

the entrance
a narrow gap
barely visible

inside hangs
fresh coolness
between high
smooth rocks

they reduce the sky
into a small blue ribbon

after each curve
sunlight falls
in various
new patterns
over the reddish walls
silence
solitude
the tracks of a cougar
in the sand

### Carson Forest

emptiness full of silence
wraps a white blanket
over meadows trees and bushes

a small creek snakes
through the valley
on the banks
clusters of aspen
wearing their winter white
stretching their branches
like bleached bones
into the deep blue sky

rolling hills
mark the valley
crowned by dark green
wilderness of firs

startled thoughts awake
full of restless yearning

## Impression of a Journey

the banks
of the river Nile
gliding by slowly
palm trees stretching
their feathery tops
into the fading sun
a camel market
is coming to an end
gold dust swirling against
the dripping light

men in long white garments
pushing and pressing
the animals on a ferry boat
lying on the bank big and broad

these men
with their elaborately tied turbans
resemble figures out of a fairy tale

# In Pharaoh's Times

solstice in Abu Simbel
priests celebrate a ceremony
in the mystic dark hall

people huddle in excitement
breathless with fear
between majestic columns

suddenly
the light slowly creeps in
dipping the stony gods
bit by bit
into glittering light
except for the god of darkness
the crowd stares in awe

thankful to their priests
who made the miracle happen again
the faithful leave the temple

## The Muezzin

tuneful singing awakens
the sleepy senses
in the grey morning at dawn
the touchy melody
sinks into the consciousness

and suddenly
memory comes back

I am in a foreign country

## Sahara

wave piles upon wave
crowned with nets of ripples
wind blows through the valleys
drives the sand through the ocean
that it might find ever new forms

the disc of the moon
sinks brightly beyond
the straight line of the horizon

before the shiny sun
appears at the opposite side
awakens the desert night
in the twilight time
with manifold voices

## Apartheid

colourfully dressed people
crowd the streets
it is market day
in Umtata

I feel uneasy
in my white skin
cannot encounter
these people
openly and freely

## In Natal

intensive the blue and green
of the landscape under me
no other colour
disturbs the double symphony
iridescent blue corresponds
the crater's lake with the sky
surrounded by the absolute green
of the picture filling
hills and meadows

while writing
making the short moment
unforgettable

## Thunderstorm

horses made out of clouds
gathered into flocks
race over the horizon
wild formations
build up voluminously

## Snake

courage
to overcome
the archaic fear
lies in touching
the cool velvet skin
in feeling the writhing strength

## Sunset

the world
everlasting spectacular
of the blazing colours
gold and orange

the slow extinguishing
of the burning disc
falling into the night

always anew
the awe
about the eternal
old farewell

## Ayers Rock

intruding the sanctuary
of the Aborigines
I stand
at the bottom of Uluru

tolerated
but not welcome

first sunrays
touch the edges
of the ravines
with their golden light
slip deeper
into brightened canyons
until the monolith
glows in red
showing majesty

the dingo waits
at the parking lot
in the outback

dropped out
of the communities
murdered by foreigners
who do good to him

# Aborigines

remembered future
destroyed
by stunted savers

## Alice Springs

an Aborigine family
stands opposite us
father mother daughter
they sold one
of their colourful paintings
to a gallery

long wiry legs
wide naked feet
made for running
rags of westerly garments

The daughter has put
a walkman on her ears

now they are standing
on the sidewalk
waiting for a taxi
to bring them home
to their dwelling

## The Search

journey after journey
and the destination
never reached

yet it lies within me

golden nets woven by the sun
into the play of the waves
fire and water
hovering over the sand

dying is beautiful
thought the little girl
looked up
to the dancing sunlight
on the moving water
alone
surrounded by bathing people

## Trees

their continual growth
put to an end
makes me reflect
about the meaning of time

## Late Summer

beautiful fragrance
of meadows
resonate to the warm waves
which mingle
with the cool breeze
they bring back memories
of all summers before

melancholy arises
makes me think of farewell

wild aromatic
elder blossom fragrance mingles
with grey-green vaporous mist
drops fall down from branches
in irregular rhythm

there is still a sense of blazing heat
broken by a tragedy

# Fall

chestnut tree
with golden leaves
full of confidence
to blossom again
next year

## Transformation

slowly falls
the autumn evening
into the silent streets

children's voices
echo in the distance

making sadness irresistible

# November

outside like inside
grey veils
press the worlds
into deep melancholy

## Age

satisfied
no more longing for an ever new spring
no more immersion in repeated summers
no more experiences of returning winters
time to go home

## Snow

flakes flutter down
soundlessly

cover kindly
remainders of autumn

fall silently
hour after hour
pile up
on trees and bushes

for a short time
the world enjoys
pristine purity

hoarfrost puts blossoms
upon the apple trees
silvery haze
lies over the valley
snow-covered mountaintops
tower behind

a new year begins